AF483540

Career Canvas

Practical Guide for Students to

Choose Right Career

Aniket Barlawar

Copyright © 2024 Aniket Barlawar

Made with ❤ on the Notion Press Platform

www.notionpress.com

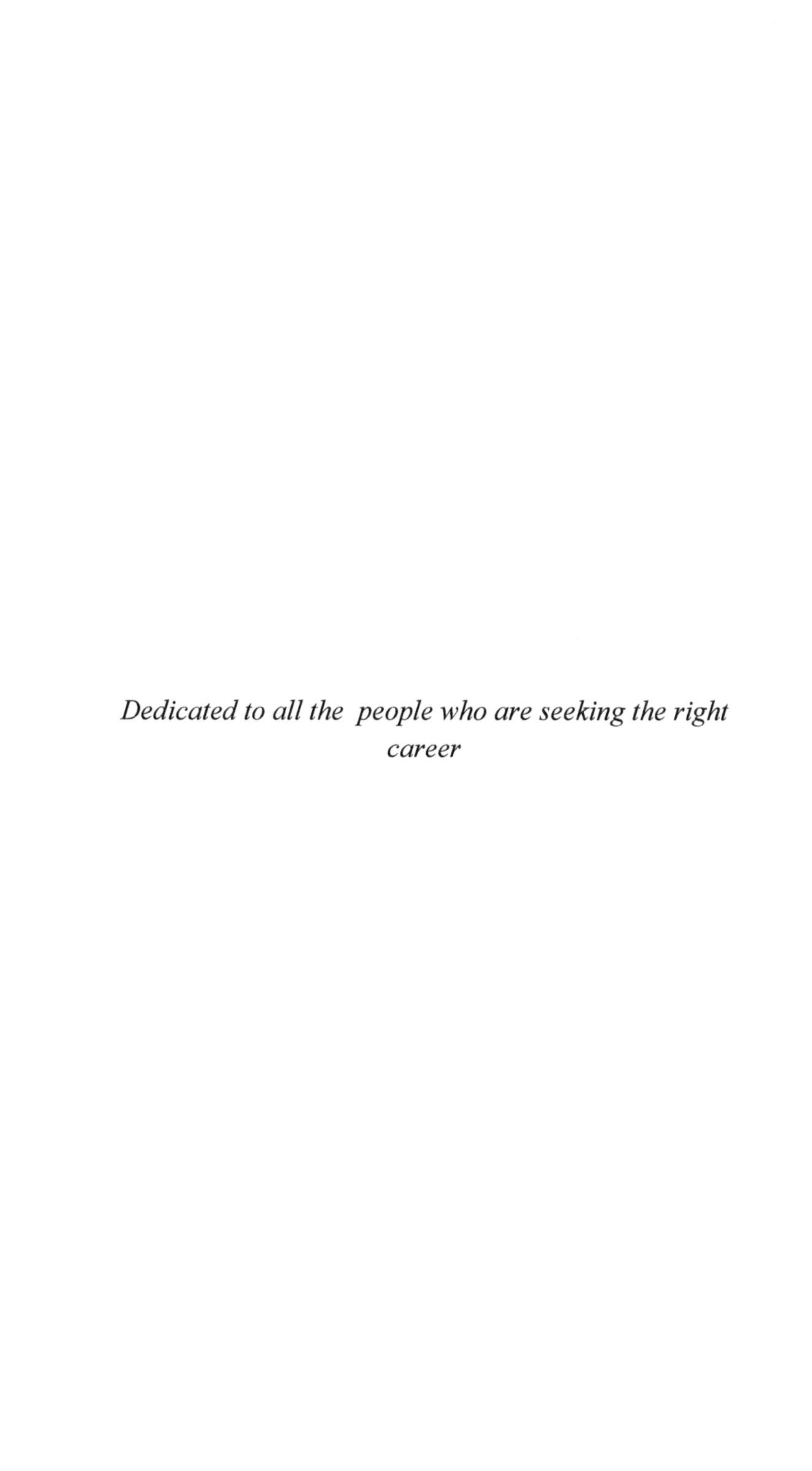

Dedicated to all the people who are seeking the right career

Contents

CONTENTS

Introduction

Welcome to "Career Canvas," your guide to navigating the wide world of career options. I am excited to be your guide as the author on this journey. This book is about choosing a right career with practical wisdom, tailored for Indian students.

Starting a career is more than just a decision; it's an important chapter in your life's story. This book serves as a beacon. It illuminates the complex and difficult process of making a wise career choice in the particular circumstances of India.

We'll go on a journey in these pages. It goes beyond common wisdom and explores the useful parts of decision-making. Our objective is to find a rewarding and meaningful career rather than just a job.

In this book, your journey begins with understanding various aspects of a career. Who influences the decision making process? Then we delve into various aspects of your personality and why this should be considered while choosing a career. With practical tools and framework, we dig deeper in understanding your interests.

With methodical approach, this book will guide you to shortlist your top career options. Finally, we will explore careers in government jobs and a career as an entrepreneur.

Remember that every person's journey is different and that there is no one-size-fits-all solution as we set out on this adventure. "Career Canvas" is more than a book. It's your friend. It offers direction and encouragement as you make decisions that will affect your future.

Who Is This Book For?

Anyone who is looking for some guidance in deciding their career, is the one who will benefit from this book. I am primarily writing this book for:

- Students
- Parents
- Teachers, who are the primary source of information for students in deciding their careers.
- And anyone who is helping students choose the right career.

This book is fantastic because it elevates the roles of many people in society who has a hand in determining one's career, such as parents, teachers, and students. My goal is to give you an understanding of how career counsellors assist students in selecting the appropriate career.

I have tried to incorporate a lot of information that I have gained over the decade of experience as a career counsellor and an HR Professional. I hope you will find it valuable too.

Why is this book different?

I wanted to gift you a practical book. A book that you can keep with you and refer to every time you are planning your career. There are many good books which are in the career sections of the library. Most of them left me more confused than I was before, plus those books have career choices that will get outdated soon. And they become obsolete.

In this book I have also shared some useful website links to help to make informed career decisions. You will also have access to a career library on our website which has updated information on latest careers.

How to Read this book?

This book is divided into 2 parts.

Part one will cover basics about a career, success, influence and many other topics. It will help you get to know you better. It will also take you through the decision-making journey.

Part 2 –career choices.

The recommended flow is read part one first before you jump into part two of the book.

Special Chapters, I have included chapters on career in Government and career as an entrepreneur.

I tried to go in depth of career in Government sector. However, the information on Government jobs are so scattered online and offline mode that must have missed few opportunities while doing my research.

Chapter on Entrepreneurship covers some of the key insights if you ever want to pursue this career choice.

Let's turn the page. Let's start an exciting journey to make wise career decisions. Today India offers many opportunities lets choose the right one for you.

Part 1

Some Basics

1. What Is A Career

You have been hearing this word a lot in your day to day world. So let's try to understand what is a career? And its various dimensions. A career is a story that you create. You do it through your decisions, actions, and accomplishments. A career is an opportunity to express yourself and learn new things. It is also a chance to change the world. It's not just a way to get money or become famous. A career is a flexible story. It can change as you find new opportunities. It is not predetermined.

Now let me tell you a story which will help you break down the above meaning of a career. There once lived a young, curious person by the name of Raghav in a world full of limitless options and pathways. Raghav had a dream, a vision of his ideal self and goals in life. His vision was his compass. It helped him navigate many options and possibilities. For him the vision was to create positive impact on the society.

Following his keen interest in cooking. He pursued a career as a chef. He started at his first job in decent 5 start hotel as a "Trainee Chef". After learning, innovating and solving challenges on the job he progressed the hierarchy of kitchen ranks and soon became Sous Chef.

His vision was to have positive impact on this society or anyone who got in touch with him. This showed up in everything that he did on the job. After becoming a Sous Chef, he realised now he has a little better resources and act on his ideas. He started exploring ways on how to make a society a better place to live. He started a small initiative, on his week offs he would cook meals for homeless elderly people and serve them on the roadsides.

This small initiative serving food consistently over the years helped him be a better person. He learned a lot from their stories. This made him a better chef since one of the responsibilities of the Chef is to also serve to the customers. This helped him grow further in his career. He became an Executive Chef or a main chef of a 5 star kitchen. With new growth he found new resources to scale his initiatives. These resources were in the form of money, people and time.

People, media started noticing this small initiative of feeding homeless elderly people. Raghav got more helping hands and other resources. This has personally helped Raghav to achieve certain Awards from the society. He was not working for those awards but they were mere by-product of efforts.

For Raghav, his work as a Chef was more than a way to support himself. It was a way to express who he is, do good, and find meaning and fulfilment. In his career every choice he made, every event he had, every chapter of his lives, it was like he was writing an epic novel. In this journey he has plot twist, surprises, and self-discovery moments.

In the end, Raghav's career was about more than just his work. It was also about the influence and legacy he left. His career was marked by achievements. He also had personal growth and the relationships he built. It was about leaving the world in a better state than when he found it. His career was about living his mark on the society.

There are many different paths one may pursue in this epic journey. Some are well-travelled career pathways, such as becoming an engineer, teacher, or doctor. Others, like being an entrepreneur, chef, or artist, were less common but no less thrilling. Raghav's story was all about his unique mix of values, skills, and interests.

You see, a career is similar to an amazing journey. It's the path one takes to fulfil their goals and desires. It's the route that an individual decides to take in order to pursue their goals, abilities, and skills.

A career is the main character in life's great story. It links a person's goals, choices, and experiences. This makes a journey of growth, both personal and professional. It has highs and lows, victories and setbacks, like any great story. But, it's a journey that adds nuance, significance, and direction to one's life's story.

The story of Raghav will help you understand what a career is, that is its an adventurous journey. Or metaphorically an individual's Journey, through work & experiences. A career is often composed of the jobs held, titles earned, and work accomplished over a long period of time.

Now let's understand the different meaning of the word "Career".

"The series of jobs that a person has in a particular area of work, usually involving more responsibility as time passes" is how the Oxford Dictionary describes a career.

According to Wikipedia, a career is a series of linked jobs. They are often in one industry or sector. For example, "a career in education" or "a career in medicine."

The Latin word carrus, which means chariot, is where the term "career" originates. It went on to signify "course of one's public or professional life" after that.

In the simplest terms, career means the part of life concerned with employment. It's the way you earn your living.

From an occupational standpoint, it means the sum of the various jobs you may hold during your lifetime.

A Career is your Journey which encompasses:

- Education
- A set of Jobs that you undertake
- Earned Title
- Achievements
- Awards.

The most significant aspect of your total identity is your career. Many people in societies are recognized by their jobs or professions. Or by their accomplishments in those fields.

You can take a pause here and visualize "How do you want your life to look like? and What will be your definition of career, consider what all things it should include – kind of Job, Lifestyle, Money, etc?"

2. What Is A Success Anyways?

When you talk about a career, the next thing many people think of is success. Oftentimes you have heard the term "Successful Career". Hence we have to discuss in brief what success means. You learned in chapter one, that career is a journey that you take for the longest period of your life.

Like a career, success is a journey. If your career is an epic adventure, then different types of success would be the milestones within that adventure. In life, success is a series of moments rather than a single event. It's about the relationships you make. It's also about the knowledge you gain and the strategies you use to get over challenges. Success is about learning from your mistakes. It is about persevering through setbacks and never giving up on your goals.

Any journey that you take will be different from any other person. Likewise, the meaning of success varies for each of us. For some, being rich is success. For others, being famous is success. And, for someone else, having power to rule is success.

There have been many studies conducted throughout the world to understand what success means. Every study shows something different. But there are also some of the common themes that I noticed in these studies on Success. We will not go into details of those studies. Let's look at the essence of what success is as I UNDERSTAND IT. (why these are in Caps because, that is my understanding and your understanding of success could be different and that totally fine.)

Success = Financial Freedom + Good Health + Happy Relationships with Family & Friends.

Let explore each of the variables here:

1. Financial Freedom:

Financial freedom is a very important aspect of living a happy life. It makes you independent & financially stable. Everybody has a different definition of financial freedom,

This is how I would like to define, "Earn enough money to get through ups and downs of life comfortably".

When I conduct career guidance sessions many students want to make a career in fields that are going to be less in demand shortly., which will directly impact their career prospects.

At the time of writing this book, the 4th industrial revolution is already underway. With the launch of

Generative AI, many jobs that exist today will not be available at all in the next 10 years.

When you make an informed decision about your career based on enough research, including the future job market, you somewhat protect yourself in a financial crisis. The job market works on simple economics that is Demand Vs Supply principle. So, if you choose a career with more demand and less supply, you will find it easy to get the jobs. These jobs will help you become financially stable and independent.

But not everyone is lucky. Without having done enough research many people end up with education that does not fetch even a single relevant job opportunity.

In early 2000, there was artificial demand created in the market for primary and secondary high school teachers. Many students who had no career plans jumped to taking up courses like Bachelor of Education (B.Ed) or Diploma in Education (D.Ed). Many educational institutes mushroomed across India to support such demands. Some were legitimate, and some were not. By the time these students finished their courses, the demand for these professionals had vanished. It was very hard for these students to find paying teacher jobs. This resulted with these graduates being unemployed for long time or working for very small salary. This also puts such graduates through mental trauma and depression.

You must have also read in the news many times that for 100 Peon/ Sweeper post lakhs of masters & Ph.D. students have applied. I would like to ask you; why do you think this is happening? When you dig deeper to understand you will find many of these applicants have taken up higher education in the field which has very limited relevance in the future job market. Hence no demand for their education qualifications.

Not all the jobs will be lost with the 4th Industrial revolutions. There will be many jobs that will be created in the future. And many jobs might stay for longer periods. You may ask which are those jobs?

Visit https://www.payscale.com/ to find out which are high paying jobs currently in the market.

2. Good Health:

The word "health" refers to a state of complete emotional and physical well-being. A healthy body & mind is essential to lead a successful life.

One of the major reasons why people are not feeling successful is because of poor health (Physically & mentally). Stress is one such factor that deteriorates mental health. Stress is what stops them from living fulfilling lives. And it is also a leading cause for many diseases, such as heart attack. Stress has also pushed many people into smoking & alcohol addiction. But why do people stress? There are many reasons and one of them is stressful career or job.

Have you heard about Monday morning blues? Stress is what happens when you don't enjoy what you are doing and drag yourself to work. When you work on something that you truly love, you don't get stressed, you feel fulfilled. If you choose a career that you don't enjoy you most likely will be stressed. And stress is not a friend of success.

3. Relationships

Relationships can be of any kind, family, friends, mentors, teachers & romantic ones. All of it in some way contributes to your success. Having a support system of your closed ones can directly affect how you perceive success.

You must have heard from our elders at home, one person is so rich but has lots of issues with family members over properties, disease or addiction. They implicitly say that person is rich but not necessarily successful.

In many interviews, successful people credit their family for their success. They thank their father, mother, friends, and spouse. This is because these people offer encouragement during hard times.

They also celebrate small milestones with you. This contributes to the overall wellbeing of an individual.

Let me add another variable to this equation to help you understand success better. In today's society success is generally associated with being Famous. For an individual that is a sign of "Recognition". But here is the challenge with being famous, it does not guarantee financial freedom, good health or happy relationships. However, it is an ego booster for sure.

Being famous or being recognized is a consequence. This is a result of actions that you take in your job, business or society.

If you are a person who values being recognized, you need to discover what recognition means to you. And dig deeper and ask yourself "why do I want recognition?". I discuss this in-depth in my coaching sessions with professionals.

The goal of this chapter was to help you understand what are variations for success and push you a little to define what success means to you.

Can you define what success means to you?

____

____

____

Tip: ask this question to your friends, family &
teachers, by doing this you will know what they
endorse as a successful life.

3. Why Choosing The Right Career Is Important?

Choosing the right career is the most important decision of your life. In the last chapters, you have learned about what is a career and what is success. You have also understood that any career is a major part of your life. And how you live your life is a result of career choices you make. Now we will know why choosing the right career is important.

Today you have an array of career choices which were not available to earlier generations. On the one hand, it is exciting to have so many possibilities. But it can also feel stressful and overwhelming. This is especially true with people unrelentingly asking, "What are you planning on doing with your life?" If you have no sense of purpose or direction, you could waste precious time in low-paying, dead-end, stressful jobs.

If you end up in the wrong job, you will waste half your energy hating it. That would harm your career and your life. Choosing the wrong career will put you in a situation. In it, you are not professionally happy or climbing the ladder of success. Your personal life will suffer.

Choosing a career path early can give you a jump-start on a bright future. Let's look at how choosing the right career positively impacts your life.

Earning Potential

If you ask why we work? The first answer is to earn good money. Choosing the correct career path sets you up for long-term financial security. Most people don't just happen to land their ideal job. They have done meticulous planning and tried to achieve their goals that they set for themselves to reach their ideal job. Very few people in the world become famous and wealthy only due to their unique talent.

For example, you might be a good artist and want to pursue Art as a career. Without enough research you took up a course in fine arts, because everyone else was suggesting that. After completion of a course you landed a decent job that pays just enough salary. With meagre salary you are just surviving and not able to afford the lifestyle you want. And you don't see any other ways to increase that income. I am sure that would be frustrating and depressing.

However, with just a little more research and after talking to right people you take up a course in Design. Which is very similar but has huge demand in the market and earning potential. I am sure your mental state will be a lot better this time.

When you look for a career, the first thing you need to do is to research career options which pay well. Then look for a career which will have the highest demand at least for the next 30 years.

The next step is shortlisting a fulfilling job with a good salary to match your personality, interests, and skills to the career you want.

Job Satisfaction

It's easier to get out of bed on a gloomy, chilly Monday morning when your job is something you enjoy. When professionals are able to meaningfully apply their skills and talents, they are most content. Job satisfaction surveys published by the Society for Human Resource Management say that 88 percent of millennials feel it's very important to work at a job that supports their career development. This is more than any other generation. A significant factor in job satisfaction is also having the respect of coworkers.

How do you gain respect in your job? Among many things, being consistently a high performer is a key aspect to gain respect in a job. You will be a high performer at your job only when you enjoy what you are doing.

Job Security

High-paying, appealing careers are within your reach if you develop a career path and follow it. A good job can greatly reduce anxiety over the high cost of living.

For example, having a job that won't go away during a recession is critical. The risk of being unemployed is greatest for unskilled jobs. Jumping around various unskilled jobs may suit some lifestyles but cost you later in terms of job security.

So, my recommendation is to build your career around high skilled jobs. They pay well and provide job security in recessions.

Stress-Free Career

We discussed stress in an earlier chapter but let us discuss a little bit more here. People who plan their career based on their interests, personality, and other things have low stress in their job.

One of the main reasons for stress is the fact that when you do not enjoy what you are doing. Many people choose a career with whatever best choice they find at a moment of making a career decision. Later in life, comes a point in their career when they really hate the profession and want to leave. Sometimes people realize this early on and are able to change their profession. In many cases people struggle to make a shift and continue with their stressful career even at the cost of their health.

In my career guidance sessions, I have met many professionals who struggle to love their job and try to find solutions for career change. You will find many such people around you, who have studied one course but are working in completely unrelated jobs.

If you are choosing a career considering your interest and personality, it will lead to a stress-free career.

Personal Life

Personal life is always impacted by your professional life and vice-versa. When you are in a career which you love, you automatically become happy. You will have high self-esteem, self-confidence, sense of achievements and fulfilment. In such a case, you will be more than happy to invest yourself mentally and emotionally in your relationships with your family & friends. Such emotional investment will bring you better support systems and help you feel fulfilled in your life. You feel more successful & content.

Finally, students who know where they are heading in life can settle into an interesting, lucrative and successful career. You need to be smart when you are making the decision about your career.

Why is it important for you to choose the right career? Write down your thoughts here.

____

____

____

"If you love what you do, you never have to work a day in your life."

4. What Influences Your Career Decisions?

Whether you agree or not, but you are always under the influence of something or someone. Which is not a bad thing. But what is important to discuss is which influences are at play when you are making a career decision.

When I was in school, I was greatly influenced by movies, every movie I have seen I wanted to be like the hero. Like, police officer, army officer, pilot, movie star and so on. Which is a good thing, but what I failed to realize then is – fantasies are fun but taking actions is what gets you a Job.

These influences can be categorized into two.

1. Internal Influences

2. External Influences

Let's explore some of **Internal Influences.**

Everybody is unique in their own. I know it sounds cliché but it is also true to the most extend. When we talk about internal influences there are few things that we need to understand.

Personality

Personality is a mix of qualities, attributes, behaviors, and thought patterns. It characterizes each person and is called their personality. It includes a range of elements, including motivations, attitudes, feelings, and social interactions. A person's personality is shaped by hereditary, environmental, and personal factors. It has a big impact on how one sees and react to the world around them.

Personality plays one of the important roles while choosing a career. Let's understand via an example. Ram is an introverted. He likes to read books and be alone. He has very few friends and does not like the company of many people. If he chooses a career where he needs to interact with people a lot on day to day job. That kind of job may be mentally draining for him.

On the other hand, Siya is an extrovert. She enjoys being outside all the time, has many friends, and enjoys spending time with people. She could be good at the same public job.

People learn and develop their personalities. This happens due to various experiences they are exposed to. Hence making career choice only based on personality is not the right way because your personality is always upgrading.

Values

Values are the ideas and standards that direct a person's actions and choices. They are the fundamental concepts that a person holds to be important and meaningful. Numerous elements, such as cultural, social, and personal experiences, can influence one's values. Examples of values are responsibility, fairness, honesty, integrity, respect, and compassion. These principles can affect how people behave with one another. They affect how people make choices and deal with different circumstances in their personal and work lives.

Values are another factor that can be considered for making a career choice. For examples, if you are someone who values "Honesty" then you will find it difficult to work in job that constantly deals with corruptions. Also, if you are someone who values "Integrity" then you might find easy to work in Armed forces.

Making a career a choice only based on Values are very difficult. But you can use this information to short list your career choices.

Interests

This is one of the Key factor in deciding the career choices. Interest are something that naturally comes to you. Seldom one can force you to develop interest. You are naturally curious about certain things in your day to day life at home, schools or even when you are alone. These interest usually stays longer with you throughout your life.

For example, if you like physics as subject, you will be pulled into reading more about it. You enjoy the experiments on Physics.

In the later part of the book I have provided you the structured way to find out your natural interests.

Now, let us look at some **external influences** on your career choices.

Parents

Parents always wants best and safe things for you. And they are the only ones who unconditionally want you to do good in life. However, let's be honest. Every parent has expectations for their child. Especially, when it comes to their child's career. Sometimes, it's very clear. But, most of the time it is implied.

Students who have their parents involved in their career decision process feel more loved and valued. However, over involvement can negatively impact a child's career decision making process. In my career counselling sessions, I have encountered parents and their children who have conflicting views on which career to choose. Though the intentions were right in these cases, having a strong opinion did not help choose the right option.

Whenever you tell your parents that you want to do a course or want to take up a profession, they will ask you "Why do you want to do this course?" This question is not to intimidate you, but they genuinely want to know. Don't give them random answers like "I have already decided" or "my friend is doing this course." Instead, explain your reason for your decision.

If you are in a place where your parents are not convinced about your career choice, here is what you can do to convince them.

- Answer yourself first, why are you choosing this career, you need to know your "WHY".
- Do enough research about the career that you want to take. Research which involves the future of such a career, what are the job opportunities, which locations or countries have such jobs and so on.
- Take up the interest assessment, one of which I have provided in this book. These

tests will help you understand your career interests.
- Talk to your parents with these points. Explain to them your "WHY". Once they know that you are serious about choosing this career and have done enough research it is easy for them to support you.

This is meant for parents only. Your views on careers and your idea of success will significantly influence your child's career choice. A common misconception among parents is that the career path that suits them may not be the best fit for their offspring. A person's career decision should be based on their preferences and one that capitalizes on your child's passions and strong points. Business and economic landscapes have changed.

The actions listed below can help you assist your children in making career decisions:

Following are the things that you can do support your children in career decision making process:

- Encourage your kids to learn more about the world around them as well as academics.
- Assist them in realizing their innate abilities and talents.
- Expand their understanding of the working world.
- Teach them how to make decisions.

- Acquire knowledge of available career resources, educational opportunities, and training programs.
- Finally, teach them how the world is evolving in business, economies & trades.

Friends

Friends are an integral part of our life, especially during the school or college days. Also, Friends can either destroy or build your career. It was in High school that I considered whether my friends were having a positive or negative effect on my life. Who we choose to surround ourselves with can have an enormous impact on who we become and how we live our lives.

Friends are the most influential people in your life when you are making career decisions. A lot of students I met during career guidance sessions have chosen to take up a career because their best friends chose that career. In my view that is the laziest & expensive way to choose a career.

When I spoke to such students, and studied deeper about such behaviour. I realized that most of these students want to just fit-in, or want to feel accepted with their peers. Every individual is unique in many ways, so is you and your friend. A career that suits your friend will not necessarily be ideal for you.

So what can you do about such influence? My recommendation is, don't take every career advice of your friends at face value and constantly question it. Your friend might hold valuable information that will be beneficial to you. Whenever you receive a suggestion of career from anyone. First research about it, collect facts and get in touch with experts who know about that particular career. Friends' influence doesn't always have to be negative if you take the right approach towards it.

Teachers

Teachers are one of the biggest influencers on students when it comes to making a career decision. For many students, teachers are their first career advisor and why not? Teachers have been tutoring their students for many years and students safely assume that their teachers know about them.

How do you know if the advice you have received from your teachers is good?

While seeking help from your teacher, see if your teacher is asking you the right questions about your interests, skills & abilities. See if a teacher knows their Why, when they suggest you any career. Is it convincing for you? I recommend going back to find more information about suggested careers.

Media (Social and Electronic)

Media is one of the influencers when you are making a career choice. I have met a student among many who wanted to be a journalist since he was heavily influenced by one of the TV anchors. I have also met many students who wanted to be an influencer on social media like Facebook, Instagram & such. There is nothing wrong in pursuing such a career. But, before taking it up, you'll have to answer this question: "Can I see myself doing this for life?". If the answer is "No" then maybe you can consider being an influencer as a hobby and continue exploring a long term career for you.

Gender

Whether we agree to it or not, gender has a major influence on our career choices. Around the world, there are various gender stereotypes at play. From a very young age, whether we like it or not we are encouraged to adhere to these gender stereotypes.

At least once in your life you must have heard, "this career is not for girls" or "oh that is women's profession. A boy should not choose that profession" or "it's not safe for women to take up that career". Be aware of such advice and stereotypes, there are no jobs which are meant only for men or women or transgender.

Financial Conditions

For many of us, money is an important influence on the future career choices. This is not surprising. We must pay for any career choice we make, whether it's an informed decision or not. How's your family financial conditions are majorly impacts your career choices. Sometimes you want to take up a course but our parents / guardians cannot support that financially. And that is Okay. You can find alternative ways to fund your education like loans, earning while learning, etc.

For example, one student I spoke to did not get good marks in NEET. He could not afford the fee of private medical colleges. So, he had to wait for another year and repeat the NEET exam. After he reappeared for the exam and failed to secure a seat in Medical college, he chose to pick up a diploma in pharmacy. But a same student from a financially well to do family may afford to get a medical seat in private college by paying a significant amount.

Financial condition may not be in your favour. But you can always find ways to achieve your goals.

Can you list down below, What & Who are influencing your Career choices?

43

____

____

____

5. What Is A Right Career After All?

Before we jump into the decision-making process let's first understand what it means by a right career. In chapter one we learned what a career is. In this chapter we will discuss what is a right career.

Right, is a word that has many meanings, in this context right means- Accurate, True, Proper & Good. Right career varies for every individual. What is right for you might not be right for someone else.

A right career suits all the aspects of your personal life. A sweet spot between what you like, what are your strengths and what the world is ready to pay for.

Let us look at it from the following diagram.

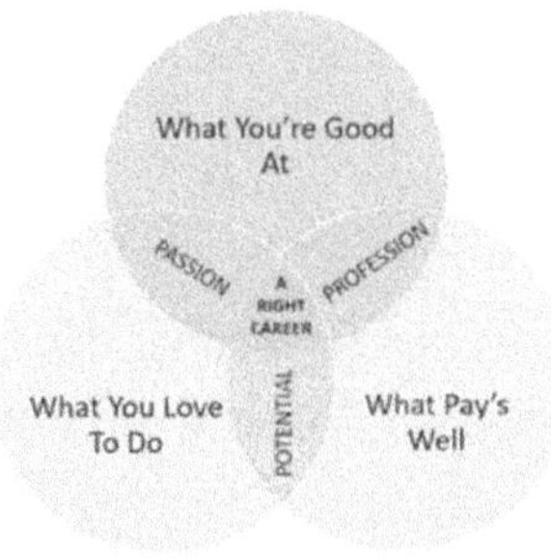

What You Love To Do

You have a great interest in something. Things you enjoy doing without any external push or motivation. And this sure sounds like a pleasurable path for a career. Who does not want to take up a hobby as a career?

Doing what you love was a mantra for many years to make career decisions. It's not wrong but neither is it correct. Choosing a career based on what you love, without considering other parameters of oneself is foolish.

For example, I played Cricket for several years until I finished my schooling. I could not wait to go to the training. I was so excited about it that I even played during my exam times. As every school kid who loves sport, I fantasized about becoming a professional. It would have been a dream to do what I loved for a living. But as honest as I can be, I was never a great player, and also lacked the resources to make it to the state teams. If I followed the advice of "Do what you love" and continued playing cricket. my life would have been completely different in some negative ways.

Knowing what you love to do is important know as this is one of the parameters to select the right career.

Let's explore what you love to do? Write down all your hobbies or things you enjoyed doing when you were a kid.

____

____

____

What You Are Good At

These are the things you may or may not enjoy doing but you are good at it. These are the things which people often ask you help on. Thigs which you do effortlessly. Which we call as Strength's. Your individual personality plays a vital role in identifying your strength or your possible strength.

Understanding and using your strengths is key. It is a cornerstone in the journey to a fulfilling and successful career. Your strengths are the areas where you excel. They show your innate abilities and skills. Finding and using these strengths is good for your growth. It is also key for making smart career choices.

"If you are good at something, take up the same career." This is the most common career advice students get. Many studies focus on the same subject. Gallup and StrengthsFinder assessments advocate this view. The problem with such career advice is that it leaves all other possibilities out of the solution of Career.

For Example: You can be good at driving two wheelers, so can you take up two wheel driving as a full time profession? Maybe not because that might not pay you well with the lifestyle you are dreaming about. But what if you are good at something and can take that skill as a career? in this case Bike Racing Sports.

Let's make a list? Write down at least two things that you are good at. How do you find out you may ask? Well it's simple, which are the things that you can do effortlessly, which are the things people compliment you for?

What Pays Well

Another career advice is to take a job that pays the bills. This rational and economical advice is behind many peoples' career decisions. If you make a career decision based on this rationale, then let me assure you: such a career might not bring you much fulfilment. You might feel disengaged in your work. But, they certainly pay the bills at the end of the month.

However, it is very important to choose a career that pays you well. Imagine you picked up a career that you love, and very good at it. But if after working for a month you end up getting salary that barely pays the bills, then you may not want to continue working in same career for long time. You will start looking for alternatives, trying to earn some extra money working overtime or taking up personal project. It might sound simple but when you are in this situation you will be frustrated, discourage and your mental health will not be sustainable in long term.

Combining the individual pieces

So far, we have only looked at the different career advice individually. Every single one has well-sounding dis-advantages and benefits. But what happens when we combine these pieces of advice? Will a new picture appear?

Passion

Passion is the overlap of your What you love to do (interests) and your What you are good at (strengths). The common career advice is to follow what we love or follow your passion.

The problem with passion is, for many it is constantly changing. What you love doing today might not like 5 years down the line.

So, should you solely follow your passion to choose a career? The likelihood of getting a right career based on only passion is quite small. It is also not wise to choose a career purely based on passion which for many is changing constantly.

There is a third piece to our diagram of career that is "What Pays Well". Suppose you follow your passion and if there is no demand for your passion? Or what if there is demand but does not pay well. Many artists fall into this category and struggle financially for example.

But it always helps to find out what your passion is at this moment in life.

Can you find out what you love and are good at? Write down below:

____

____

____

Profession

Profession is where our strengths meet the willingness of others to pay for it. Our whole business world is built on that idea. Remember Demand Vs Supply economics from Chapter two?

We get paid for what skills we can offer. At the same time, we pay others for things we are not good at or do not want to do.

In my counseling practice, I have observed that most of the people are operating in a profession. We get educated in universities and schools to learn general skills necessary for the business world.

This all is done to simply exchange our skills for the most money. It is a basic equation. The problem is that it is completely rational. There are no interests or passions involved, which means you will not necessarily enjoy what you are doing. But you have enough money to live a comfortable life.

Is this bad? Not necessarily. If you are someone who prefers to be only in an professions that just pays well so that you can fulfil your materialist dreams. This is good option.

Can you find out what you are good at & pays well? Write down below:

____

____

____

Potential

When we love doing something and the world is willing to pay for it, then we possess potential. But remember, you love doing it but you are not naturally good at it. What happens if we choose a career based on just potential, we underestimate the amount of hard work you need to put in to make it a right career.

Let's explore this idea with an example. You really want to be a doctor, but if you are not good at Biology as a subject, you will have to put a lot of effort to build your skills in this subject.

The tremendous possibility with Potential is skills can always be developed; you just need to work harder.

Can you find out what you love doing & pays well? Write down below:

____

____

____

The whole picture

Slowly a clear picture is emerging. You have seen that your interests are a good indicator for what career you should follow. At the same time, you also learned about general economics of career. As can be seen from the diagram when you do something you are good at, which interests you and you get paid for it then you find yourself in **The Right Career**. It gives you everything you need.

Part 2

Career Assessment

6. Free Career Interest Assessment

Your Free Career Interest Assessment

As I promised, here is our free online career interest assessment that measures your interests, and personality. This free assessment is based on Holland's Codes (RIASEC) which was developed by psychologist John L. Holland in the 1970s. Dr. Holland reasoned that people work best in work environments that match their interests.

Holland Codes are one of the most popular models used for career tests today. Holland argued that the choice of a career is an expression of personality. There are six personality types in Holland's model and most people will fit into a few of the categories.

I have been using RAISEC career assessment with other assessment to discover the career interest for the students.

58

I like to work on cars	○					
I like to do puzzles		○				
I am good at working independently			○			
I like to work in teams				○		
I am an ambitious person, I set goals for myself					○	
I like to organize things, (files, desks/offices)						○
I like to build things	○					
I like to read about art and music			○			
I like to have clear instructions to follow						○
I like to try to influence or persuade people					○	
I like to do experiments		○				
I like to teach or train people				○		
I like trying to help people solve their problems				○		
I like to take care of animals	○					
I wouldn't mind working 8 hours per day in an office						○
I like selling things					○	
I enjoy creative writing			○			
I enjoy science		○				
I am quick to take on new responsibilities					○	
I am interested in healing people				○		
I enjoy trying to figure out how things work		○				

	R	I	A	S	E	C
I like putting things together or assembling things	◯					
I am a creative person			◯			
I pay attention to details						◯
I like to do filing or typing						◯
I like to analyze things (problems/ situations)		◯				
I like to play instruments or sing			◯			
I enjoy learning about other cultures				◯		
I would like to start my own business					◯	
I like to cook	◯					
I like acting in plays			◯			
I am a practical person	◯					
I like working with numbers or charts		◯				
I like to get into discussions about issues				◯		
I am good at keeping records of my work						◯
I like to lead					◯	
I like working outdoors	◯					
I would like to work in an office						◯
I'm good at math		◯				
I like helping people				◯		
I like to draw			◯			
I like to give speeches					◯	

	R	I	A	S	E	C
Grand Total						
Holland Codes	R	I	A	S	E	C

Add up the number of filled in circles in each column for a grand total.

Take the three letters with the highest scores and record them under "My Interest Code".

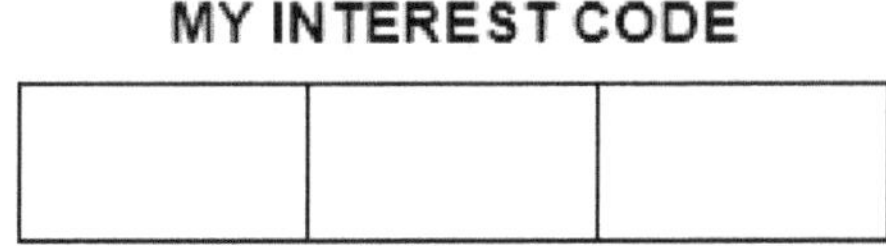

How to interpret above test result

Your top three interests are represented by this code. The first letter of the interest code is your top preference. The second letter is your second preference, where your interest is lesser than first code but a little higher than third code. Your third code is lesser preferred and higher than rest of the 3 letters which did not make it to the top list.

For example, if your interest code is "RES," for instance, you would most closely resemble the Realistic type, somewhat less so the Enterprising type, and even less so the Social type.

Career choices based on the first letter will be more suitable for you, followed by second letter related career options and last career choices should be from third letter related career options.

To illustrate, if you interest code is "IER", then career choices from "Investigative" options are more suitable for you then followed by "Enterprising" and last from "Realistic"

DO NOT TRY TO FIND THE EXACT MATCH WITH YOUR CAREER INTEREST CODES. This will limit your career choices to just one or two.

Please note that I have tried to provide as many as possible career options for each of the codes in part II of this book. However, this is not an exhaustive list and many career options may be excluded since they are not very popular.

7. Career Options

*The greatest happiness comes from absorbing
yourself in some goal outside yourself."*

– Richard Layard

R: Realistic (Doers)

A realistic personality type enjoys working with
hands to explore the world and accomplish things.
These individuals are mostly interested in jobs that
require working with tools, machines, and physical
skills. What we generally call a hands on Approach.
They are builders, they like building things. They
prefer working with tangible things, such as tools,
machines, plants, and animals rather than with
ideas, data, and people.

Typical traits of Realistic people are:

Practical, athletic, straightforward/frank,
mechanically inclined, a nature lover, thrifty,
curious about the physical world, stable, concrete,
reserved, self-controlled, independent, ambitious,
systematic, persistent, etc.

Realistic people like to:

Tinker with machines/vehicles, work outdoors, use your hands, be physically active, build things, tend/train animals, work on equipment, etc.

Following are some of the Career options where Realistic people can thrive.

Aerospace Physiologist (RSE)

Air-Conditioning Mechanics (RIE)

Aircraft Mechanic (RIE)

Appliance Mechanics (RIE)

Aqua culturist (REI)

Architect (RAI)

Architectural Drafter (RCI)

Automotive Engineer (RIE)

Automobile Mechanic (RIE)

Baker/Chef (RSE)

Biomedical Engineer (RAI)

Compositor (RSI)

Civil Engineer (REC)

Police Officer (RES)

Dental Assistant (RES)

Dental Laboratory Technician (REC)

Dental Technician (REI)

Electrical Engineer (RIE)

Electrician (RES)

Farmer (RIS)

Farm Manager (RES)

Fiber Optics Technician (RSE)

Firefighter (RES)

Fish Hatchery Manager (RES)

Floral Designer (RAE)

Forester (RIS)

Geodetic Surveyor (RIE)

Industrial Supervisor (REI)

Jeweler (REC)

Laboratory Technician (RIE)

Mechanical Engineer (RIS)

Metallurgical Technician (RIS)

Oceanographer (RIE)

Optician (REI)

Petroleum Engineer (RIE)

Nurse (RSE)

Property Manager (RES)

Quality Control Manager (RSE)

Renewable Energy Engineer (RIA)

Sailor (REC)

I: Investigative (Thinkers)

An investigative personality type tends to be analytical, intellectual and scholarly. They enjoy research, mathematical or scientific activities. These individuals live in their mind and prefer to deal with the real world from a distance. They like to read, study, use books and other data instead of working hands-on. These individuals are unconventional and independent thinkers, who are curious and very insightful. There are the people who prefer to work with **"data"**. They like to "think and observe rather than act, to organize and understand information rather than to persuade". They also prefer "individual rather than people-oriented activities".

The typical traits of the Investigative people are:

Inquisitive, analytical, scientific, observant, precise, scholarly, cautious, intellectually self-confident, introspective, reserved, broad-minded, independent, logical, complex, curious, etc.

Investigative people like to:

Explore a variety of ideas, play computers Games, work independently, perform lab experiments, read scientific or technical journals, analyze data, deal with abstractions, do research, and be challenged.

Following are some of the Career options where Investigative people can thrive.

Actuary (ISE)

Agronomist (IRS)

Air Traffic Controller (IRS)

Anaesthesiologist (IRS)

Anthropologist (IRE)

Archaeologist (IRE)

Astrophysicist (IRS)

Biochemist (IRE)

Biologist (ISR)

Biotechnologist (IAE)

Biomedical Researcher (IAE)

Blockchain Developer (IAE)

Cartographer (IRE)

Chemical Engineer (IRE)

Chemist (IRE)

Chiropractor (ISR)

Civil Engineer (IRS)

Computer Engineer (IRC)

Software Developer (IAR)

Computer Systems Analyst (IER)

Cybersecurity Analyst (IRS)

Data Scientist (IAE)

Doctor (IAS)

Dentist (ISR)

Disaster Management Specialist (IRS)

Ecologist (IRE)

Environmental Scientist – (IAE)

Economist (ISA)

Electrical Engineer (IRE)

Ethical Hacker (IRE)

Ethnographer (IAE)

Forensic Scientist (IRS)

Food Technologist (IAE)

Geographer (IRE)

Geologist (IRE)

Game Developer (IAE)

Genetic Counsellor (IAE)

GIS Specialist (IRS)

Horticulturist (IRS)

Industrial Arts Teacher (IER)

Management Consultant (ICR)

Marketing Research Analyst (IAS)

Marine Biologist (IRS)

Mathematician (IER)

Medical Lab Technologist (IRE)

Meteorologist (IRS)

Microbiologist (IAE)

Mobile App Developer (IAE)

Nanotechnologist (IAE)

Nurse (ISA)

Neuroscientist (IRS)

Pharmacist (IES)

Doctor, General Practice (ISE)

Physician Assistant (ISA)

Psychologist (ISA)

Patent Analyst (IAE)

Radiologist (IAS)

Research Analyst (IRC)

Robotics Engineer (IRE)

Solar Energy Consultant (IAE)

Software Engineer (IRE)

Software Tester (IAC)

Statistician (IRE)

Sustainability Consultant (IRS)

Technical Writer (IRS)

Urban Planner (IRS)

Veterinary Doctor (IRS)

Web Site Developer (IRE)

Wildlife Conservationist (IRS)

A: Artistic (Creators)

An artistic personality type uses their hands and mind to create new things. They appreciate beauty, unstructured activities and variety. They enjoy interesting and unusual people, sights, textures and sounds. These individuals prefer to work in unstructured situations and use their **creativity and imagination**. They tend to be "creative, open, inventive, original, perceptive, sensitive, independent and emotional". They rebel against "structure and rules", but enjoy "tasks involving people or physical skills". They tend to be more emotional than the other types.

Typical traits of Artistic people are:

Creative, intuitive, imaginative, innovative, unconventional, emotional, independent, expressive, original, introspective, impulsive, sensitive, courageous, open, complicated, idealistic, and nonconforming.

Artistic people like to:

Attend concerts, theatres, art exhibits, read fiction, plays, and poetry, work on crafts, take photographs, express yourself creatively, deal with ambiguous ideas, etc.

Following are some of the career options Artistic people can thrive in.

Actor/Actress (AES)

Advertising Art Director (AES)

Advertising Manager (ASE)

Architect (AIR)

Animator (AER)

Chef/Culinary Expert (ARE)

Clothing/Fashion Designer (ASR)

Copywriter (ASI)

Content Writer (AIE)

Dancer (AES)

Digital Marketing Specialist – (AIS)

Digital Illustrator (AER)

Choreographer (AER)

Drama Teacher (ASE)

English Teacher (ASE)

Fashion Illustrator (ASR)

Fashion Designer (ARE)

Furniture Designer (AES)

Food Blogger/Influencer (ASE)

Graphic Designer (AES)

Human Rights Activist (SEA)

Interior Designer (AES)

Journalist/Reporter (ASE)

Landscape Architect (AIR)

Medical Illustrator (AIE)

Museum Curator (AES)

Music Teacher (AES)

Photographer (AES)

Sound Engineer (AER)

Social Media Manager (ASE)

UX/UI Designer (AER)

Voice-over Artist (AES)

Writers/Editors (ASI)

S: Social (Helpers)

Individuals who are a social personality type are dedicated leaders, humanistic, responsible and supportive. They use feelings, words and ideas to work with people rather than physical activity to do things. They enjoy closeness, sharing, groups, unstructured activity and being in charge. People who like to work with **"people"** and who "seem to satisfy their needs in teaching or helping situations". They tend to be "drawn more to seek close relationships with other people and are less apt to want to be really intellectual or physical".

Typical traits of Social people are:

Friendly, helpful, idealistic, insightful, outgoing, understanding, cooperative, generous, responsible, forgiving, patient, empathic, kind, persuasive, etc.

Social people like to:

Work in groups, help people with problems, participate in meetings, do volunteer work, work with young people, play team sports, serve others, get involved in solving disputes.

Following are some of the career options Social people can thrive in.

Air Traffic Controller (SER)

Athletic Trainer (SRE)

Art Therapist (AER)

City Manager (SEC)

College Professor (SEI)

Community Manager (SEA)

Counseling Psychologist (SIA)

Counselor/Therapist (SAE)

Cosmetologist (SEA)

Cruise Director (SAE)

Dental Hygienist (SAI)

Detective (SER)

Dietitian (SIE)

Elementary School Teacher (SEC)

Event Planner (SAE)

Fitness Trainer (SAE)

Hairstylist (SER)

High School Teacher (SAE)

Historian (SEI)

Hospital Administrator (SER)

Hotel Management Professional (SAE)

Organizational Psychologist (SEI)

Insurance Claims Examiner (SIE)

Industrial Psychologist (SEA)

Intellectual Property Lawyer (SEA)

Librarian (SAI)

Lawyer (SEA)

Medical Assistant (SCR)

Medical Record Administrator (SIE)

Politician/Minister (SAI)

Priest(SAI)

Nurse/Midwife (SIR)

Occupational Therapist (SRE)

Paralegal (SCE)

Park Naturalist (SEI)

Human Resources / Personnel, Training, and Labor Relations Specialist(SEC)

Physiotherapist (SIE)

Pharmacist (SIA)

Police Officer (SER)

Preschool Worker (SEA)

Public Health Educator (SEA)

Psychologist (SAI)

Radiological Technologist (SRI)

Real Estate Appraiser (SCE)

Recreation Director (SER)

Social Worker (SAI)

Sports Coach/Trainer (SAE)

Speech Therapist (SAI)

Aniket Barlawar

E: Enterprising (Persuaders)

What is an enterprising person? These individuals like to work with people, influence, persuade, lead or manage for organizational goals or economic gain. An enterprising personality type is often a leader who is talented at organizing, persuading and managing. They enjoy money, power, status and being in charge. People who like to work with **"people and data"**. They tend to be "good talkers, and use this skill to lead or persuade others". They "also value reputation, power, money and status".

Typical traits of Enterprising people are:

Self-confident, assertive, sociable, persuasive, enthusiastic, energetic, adventurous, popular, impulsive, ambitious, inquisitive, agreeable, talkative, extroverted, spontaneous, optimistic, etc.

Enterprising people like to:

Initiate projects, convince people to do things their way, sell things or promote ideas, give talks or speeches, organize activities, lead a group, Make decisions affecting others, be elected to office, win a leadership or sales award, start their own service or business, campaign politically, meet important people, have power or status, etc.

Following are some of the career options
Enterprising people can thrive in.

Advertising, marketing, and public relations
managers (ESA)

Advertising/ Sales Representative (ESR)

Hairdresser (ESR)

Bartender (ERC)

Business Analyst (EAI)

Benefits Manager (ESA)

Financial Manager (ESA)

Financial Analyst (EAI)

Financial Planner (EAI)

Insurance Adjuster (ESR)

Investment Analyst (EAI)

Investment Banker (EAI)

Computer Operator (ESI)

Chef (ESR)

Chartered Accountant (EAC)

Credit Analyst (EAS)

Credit Manager (ERS)

Educational - Training Manager (EIS)

Educational Administrator (ESA)

Flight Attendant (ESA)

Food Service Manager (ESI)

Foreign Service Officer (ESA)

Health Services Manager (ECR)

Hotel Manager (ESR)

Industrial Engineer (EIR)

Insurance Agent (ECS)

Interpreter (ESA)

Journalism (EAS)

Lawyer/Attorney (ESA)

Market Research Analyst (EIA)

Office Manager (ESR)

Human Resources Manager (EAS)

Public Relations Representative (EAS)

Real Estate Agent (ESR)

Restaurant Manager (EAS)

Retail Store Manager (ESR)

Sales Manager (ESA)

Sales Representative (ERS)

Social Service Director (ESA)

Stockbroker (ESI)

Tax Accountant (ECS)

Traffic Clerks (ESC)

Travel Agent (ECS)

Urban Planner (ESI)

Marketing Manager (EAC)

C: Conventional (Organizers)

A **conventional personality type** likes to work with data and numbers, carry out tasks in detail and follow through on the instructions of others. They are quiet, careful, responsible, well organized and task oriented. These individuals use their mind, eyes and hands to carry out tasks. People who prefer to work with **"data"** and who "like rules and regulations and emphasize self-control ... they like structure and order, and dislike unstructured or unclear work and interpersonal situations". They also "place value on reputation, power, or status".

Typical traits of Conventional people are:

Well-organized, accurate, numerically inclined, methodical, conscientious, efficient, conforming, orderly, practical, thrifty, systematic, structured, polite, ambitious, obedient, persistent, etc.

Conventional people like to:

Follow clearly defined procedures, use data processing equipment, work with numbers type or take shorthand, be responsible for details, collect or organize things, etc.

Following are some of the career options Enterprising people can thrive in.

Abstractor (CSI)

Accountant (CSE)

Accounting Clerk and Bookkeeper (CSR)

Administrative Assistant (ESC)

Bank Teller (CSE)

Budget Analyst (CER)

Building Inspector (CSE)

Business Teacher (CSE)

Cashier (CSE)

Clerk (CSE)

Computer Operator (CSR)

Cost Accountant (CES)

Court Reporter (CSE)

Customs Inspector (CEI)

Data processing worker (CRI)

Financial Analyst (CSI)

Insurance Adjuster (CSE)

Insurance Underwriter (CSE)

Kindergarten Teacher (CSE)

Legal Secretary (CSA)

Library Assistant (CSE)

Medical Records Technician (CSE)

Medical Secretary (CES)

Safety Inspector (RCS)

Service Station Attendant (CER)

Tax Consultant (CES)

Telephone Operator (CSE)

Typist (CES)

8. Choosing A Right Career

"If you care about what people think about you, you will end up being their slave. Reject and pull your own rope." — **Auliq Ice**

Now that you know what is your interest code is and related career options available for these codes. I encourage you to visit **https://careersage.edumilestones.com/**. And research on each of your shortlisted careers on this website. Career information is updated very often on our website so that you get the latest information on each career choices.

You will find many options under each of the Holland code Careers. Read each career description carefully and choose top 5 career options that excite you. Next step is write them on table shared on the next pages. This will ensure that you will have all necessary information to make an informed decision.

Career Canvas

Option 1:	
Education Tenure (*in Years*)	
Job Demand (low-med-high)	
Your Interest Level (low-med-high)	
Level of Preparation (low-med-high)	
Benefits (to me, Family, Society)	
Cost (Me & Family)	
Lifestyle (Does it provide the lifestyle I want to have in future)	
Pros of this career choice	
Cons of this career choice	

Option 2:	
Education Tenure (*in Years*)	
Job Demand (low-med-high)	
Your Interest Level (low-med-high)	
Level of Preparation (low-med-high)	
Benefits (to me, Family, Society)	
Cost (Me & Family)	
Lifestyle (Does it provide the lifestyle I want to have in future)	
Pros of this career choice	
Cons of this career choice	

Career Canvas

Option 3:	
Education Tenure (*in Years*)	92
Job Demand (low-med-high)	
Your Interest Level (low-med-high)	
Level of Preparation (low-med-high)	
Benefits (to me, Family, Society)	
Cost (Me & Family)	
Lifestyle (Does it provide the lifestyle I want to have In future)	
Pros of this career choice	
Cons of this career choice	

Option 4:	
Education Tenure (*in Years*)	
Job Demand (low-med-high)	
Your Interest Level (low-med-high)	
Level of Preparation (low-med-high)	
Benefits (to me, Family, Society)	
Cost (Me & Family)	
Lifestyle (Does it provide the lifestyle I want to have in future)	
Pros of this career choice	
Cons of this career choice	

Career Canvas

Option 5:	
Education Tenure (*in Years*)	94
Job Demand (low-med-high)	
Your Interest Level (low-med-high)	
Level of Preparation (low-med-high)	
Benefits (to me, Family, Society)	
Cost (Me & Family)	
Lifestyle (Does it provide the lifestyle I want to have in future)	
Pros of this career choice	
Cons of this career choice	

Make A Decision

"On an important decision one rarely has 100% of the information needed for a good decision no matter how much one spends or how long one waits. And, if one waits too long, he has a different problem and has to start all over. This is the terrible dilemma of the hesitant decision maker."

— Robert K. Greenleaf, The Servant as Leader

Most majority decisions lack systematic thought. They also lack critical thinking.

Confidence to make a decision comes from clarity. You achieve clarity when you have most of the relevant information. With previous exercises you eliminated all the noises around career choices. You have built the confidence and clarity to decide. This is what we call an informed decision-making process.

Are you still hesitant to decide? What are your unanswered questions?

Write down your unanswered questions below. Seek the answers from your family, friends, or professional career counselor.

Question: ______________________________________

Answer: ______________________________________

Question: ______________________________________

Answer: ______________________________________

Once you have all the answers, go to the next step and rank your career options in priority. Consider all the information you have gathered about each of the five career options in previous exercise.

With your new found knowledge of each career option, rank your career choices from one (Most favourite) to Five (Least favourite). You can always change the ranking if you acquire more information about your career options.

1st ______________________________

2nd ______________________________

3rd ______________________________

4th ______________________________

5th ______________________________

Great Job!!! Now you have a top career option that suits your interests, Personality, and has a great job opportunity.

Review the decision

Congratulations!!! For deciding the top career choice. I know this whole exercise could have been challenging for you. A wise career decision is most of the time followed through gaining more insights on choices.

I am happy that you were able to make a head start with it.

The decision-making process, like a recipe, does not stop at a decision. Your next step is to review the decision, like how you give a prepared dish for tasting.

Consider your 1st i.e. Most Favorite Career Choice. I have prepared a few questions for you that will help you validate your choice.

Answer following questions as specific and detailed as possible. After all you are your best critic isn't it?

How Do I feel now?

____

How did my family & friends react to my choice? Please "WHY" they liked or disliked the choice

____

Am I satisfied with my Choice

____

98

Am I confident with my Choice

____

What do you think is missing from your choosen careerand are you okay with it

____

Take Action

Once you have decided which career you want to choose and feel confident & happy about your choice. It's time to focus your energy on further exploration into Courses, colleges, Universities, Entrance Exams, job placements and so on. I will help you few guiding question below to help you dig deeper.

Which are the best colleges/ universities you can take these courses?

Which entrance exams do you need to crack to get admitted to these colleges? & what is the level of preparation for entrance exams?

Are there any college / university specific entrance exams?

What are the timelines to apply for these colleges?

What is the admission process?

Do I know anyone from this profession / College / University? Can I connect to them through social media/ personal contacts?

What is the college's track record in job placements?

What extracurricular activities that you can participate in?

Will this degree help me apply for government jobs or make me eligible for further studies?

Our website https://careersage.edumilestones.com/ will help you answer a lot of the above questions.

Still not Sure?

I understand your dilemma. Career Indecision is a challenge for many people. I have guided many Students and professionals during career counselling sessions who suffer from career indecisions. Not taking a decision is also a decision. If you don't take decision for yourself then you will be forced to follow someone else's decision for you.

This is due to many reasons. Some include: lack of information, uncertainty, hidden influences, fear of commitment, and more. In my experience I have found that students delay making decisions until the very last minutes. Then under pressure from family, society, and friends they get pushed into a career that they do not feel belonging to. This can be frustrating, energy sucking and costly mistake for oneself.

If you are at this stage right now, you are not alone. But I would recommend getting help from a professional career counselor. After all you will be spending a large amount of your productive time and money in building your career.

9. Career As An Entrepreneurs

Entrepreneurship is the process of creating, launching, and running a new business venture. It involves taking risks, innovating, and solving problems. Entrepreneurship can be a rewarding career option for those who have a passion for their ideas and a vision for their future. Entrepreneurship can also help a country develop economically and socially. It does so by creating jobs, making wealth, and addressing social problems.

A report by Global Entrepreneurship Monitor says India ranked third. This was among 54 countries in early-stage entrepreneurial activity in 2020. The rise for such entrepreneurship spirit in India is also due to many government schemes. These include StartUp India, Make in India, Atal Innovation Mission, and Atmanirbhar Bharat.

India has a large and diverse population, a growing middle class, a supportive government, and a vibrant startup ecosystem. These factors make India an attractive destination for aspiring entrepreneurs.

Some of the benefits of pursuing entrepreneurship as a career in India are:

- You can pursue your passion and interests, and work on something that you love and believe in.
- You can have more autonomy and flexibility, and set your own goals and schedules.
- You can learn new skills and gain valuable experience, by facing challenges and overcoming obstacles.
- You can create a positive impact, by solving problems, fulfilling needs, and improving lives.
- You can achieve financial independence and growth, by generating revenue and profits.
- Some of the challenges of pursuing entrepreneurship as a career in India are:
- You have to face uncertainty and risk, and deal with failures and setbacks.
- You have to invest a lot of time, money, and resources, and manage multiple aspects of your business.
- You have to compete with other players, and cope with changing market conditions and customer preferences.
- You have to deal with legal, regulatory, and ethical issues, and comply with rules and standards.
- You have to balance your personal and professional life, and handle stress and pressure.

How to be an entrepreneur?

Well, there is no specific course or degree that you can complete and call yourself an Entrepreneur. Then how can you be an entrepreneur? For the sake of simplicity I can say build a business. To build a business, you need to find the problem that a society or group is facing. Then, you should solve their problem with technology, products, or processes.

However, to be an entrepreneur is easier said than being one. You need a variety of skills to be a successful entrepreneur. I am listing few of them below

Certainly, here are the key skills required to be an entrepreneur in bullet points:

- Vision and Creativity

- Decision-Making

- Risk Management

- Adaptability

- Leadership

- Communication Skills

- Financial Literacy

- Time Management

- Networking

- Sales and Marketing

- Negotiation Skills

- Customer Focus

- Problem-Solving

- Resource Management

- Tech Savvy

- Resilience

- Emotional Intelligence

- Continuous Learning

I know this is a long list. But, you don't need all to start. But, you need them to be successful.

There are many courses available in the market to train you on these skills, the most popular being MBA in Entrepreneurship. There are also a lot of short duration courses available in offline & online mode with free to few lakhs in fees.

10. Career In Government

A government job is when you work for a central or state government or its agencies or companies. For many students in India, getting a government job is their top goal. It is one of the safest careers for financial security. It offers great perks and status. At the same time, it lets you have a big impact on people's lives.

Let's explore in details pros & cons of working for the Government.

Stability and Job Security

Pros

- Government jobs in India are often considered stable and offer job security.
- Government employees are entitled to various benefits which includes lifelong pension and gratuities. This enable one to feel financially safe during the old age.
- Lower chances of getting laid off due to economic or reasons.

Cons

- Career progression may be slower in government jobs.

- The rigid hierarchical structure can be limiting for career progression.

Compensation and Benefits

Pros

- Government jobs frequently come with competitive payment packages and allowances.
- The benefits are like those of health insurance and travel allowances. They are better than those of many private companies.
- Pay raises are standard across the pay grades. Regular pay commission revisions greatly increase the salary. This is irrespective of one's performance.

Cons

- A lot of time salaries are paid in arrears that irregular payments.
- Compliance requirements & regulatory needs often delays the payouts.
- Compared to some of the private sector jobs salary may look lesser for government workers.

Work- Life Balance

Pros

- Government jobs generally have standard working hours. This contributing to a better work- life balance.
- Holidays / Leaves are generally well-defined. They are more in numbers compared to private sector employees. Leave approvals are easy & flexible.
- In certain conditions one can avail extended leaves without leaving the job. This is not possible in private sector jobs.

Cons

- Some government jobs require being available 24/7. Anyone can be called to serve the public during emergencies like war, flood, and elections.

Career Growth and Advancement

Pros

- Opportunities for career growth are well defined and available through departmental examinations. Which eliminates the personal biases of leadership in promotions.

- The government frequently invests in the training and development of its workers.

Cons

- Advancement may occasionally be slow, and competition for advanced positions can be fierce.
- Career progression may be subject to regulatory processes.

Job Diversity and openings

Pros

- Government jobs are available in variety of sectors. This offers a wide range of career options.
- Job openings are available for different educational qualifications. You can start your career at the entry level or mid-level. Or, as a Class 1 officer, depending on the exams you clear.

Cons

- The selection processes is competitive, making it challenging to secure a government job.

- You can't apply for all the government jobs as some may require specific qualifications.

Job Satisfaction and Social Impact

Pros

- Numerous government jobs give opportunities to contribute to the welfare of society.
- Job opportunities in areas like public services, healthcare, and education can be very satisfying.
- Most of the government jobs brings a good status to the individual in society.

Cons

- Regulatory processes hamper quick decision
- Certain jobs may involve dealing with red tapism, Corruption and political influence.

Educational Qualifications and Entry Conditions

Pros

- Government jobs have clear entry conditions. This makes it easy for candidates to understand who is eligible.
- Competitive examinations are structured, furnishing equal opportunities for good candidates.

Cons

- The process of preparing for competitive examinations can be time- consuming and challenging.
- Certain jobs may have strict age limits for eligibility.
- Most of the job opportunities are also based on reservations.

A career in government jobs in India presents a blend of advantages and challenges. Stability, job security, and chances for social impact are some of the charms. However, its heavy regulations, slow career progression, and fierce competition are factors to consider during selection.

In the end, the choice is between a government job and a career in the private sector. It depends on personal preferences, career goals, and values.

If you are one of those aspirants, then you need to understand who are the various employers who offer government jobs in India. Let's explore them together.

Many types of government jobs are available. They are with the Union Public Service Commission, Staff Selection Commission, state public service commissions, Indian Railways & metros, public sector undertakings, defence services, Government education institutions, Universities, banking, and other financial sectors.

Each of these jobs has different eligibility criteria, selection process and career prospects.

Following are some of the top government jobs in India are

Civil Services:

These are all India Jobs. The government of India fills them via UPSC. These jobs include the Indian Administrative Service (IAS), Indian Foreign Service (IFS), Indian Police Service (IPS), and other central services. Civil servants enforce government programs, maintain law and order, represent India internationally, and carry out executive functions. To qualify for civil service roles, you must pass the UPSC exams, which have three stages: primary, mains, and interview.

State Public Service Commission (SPSC):

Like UPSC every state has their own Public Service Commission. For example, Maharashtra Public Service Commission, Tamilnadu Public Service Commission, etc. These are state position civil services that deal with the administration and governance of the separate states. SPSCs conduct examinations for various posts similar as state executive service, state police service, state revenue service, etc. SPSCs offer similar benefits and challenges as the Indian civil services, but with a focus and compass on the specific states.

Public Sector Undertakings (PSUs)

These are government-owned companies that operate in various sectors such as oil and gas, power, mining, and telecom. PSUs offer workers gratuities, and other benefits. They also provide opportunities for growth and development. Some of the top PSUs are ONGC, NTPC, IOCL, BHEL, and SAIL. PSUs hire workers through exams like GATE, UGC NET, and CAT. They also hire through campus placements.

Defence Services

Career opportunities in Defence sector can be broadly categorized into two.

1. Indian Armed Forces, which include the Indian Army, Indian Navy, Indian Air Force, and Indian Coast Guard.
2. Central Armed Forces which includes CISF (Central Industrial Security Force), CRPF (Central Reserve Police Force), ITPB (Indo Tibetan Border Police), SSB (Sashastra Seema Bal)

Defence services are responsible for guarding the sovereignty and integrity of the nation. Defence personnel also work for various peacekeeping and philanthropic operations. Defence services offer a prestigious and audacious career. These services offer variety of allowances, Benefits, lifestyle and social status.

Defence services hire employees through mainly through two channels.

1. Through UPSC examinations like NDA (National Defence Academy), CDSE (Combined Defence Services Examination), SSC (Short Service Commission).
2. Through direct Entry.

Government Teachers or University Professor

These are academic positions in government-run schools or universities. The employees teach, explore, and mentor students. Government teachers or professors enjoy academic freedom, intellectual stimulation, and respect in the society. They also get decent salaries, pensions, and other benefits. The government hires teachers and professors through exams like UGC NET, CSIR NET, and SET. Or, they hire them directly for separate institutions.

Indian Railways

These are specialized positions in the Indian Railroads, which is one of the largest and most complex rail networks in the world. Railways are responsible for designing, building, and running parts of the rail system. This includes tracks, platforms, signals, trains, and more. Railways pay employees good salaries, and allowances. They also gets opportunities to travel the whole India. Railway employees are hired through two channels

1. You can join Indian Railways as a Class 1 or Group A officer via the UPSC (Civil Services Examination) / Indian Engineering Services (IES) examination.

2. For Group B, C & D recruitment is done via Railway Recruitment Board (RRB) or through GATE Scores.

Bank Job

These are job opportunities in various positions of public sector banks, State Bank of India (SBI), Punjab National Bank (PNB), Bank of Baroda (BOB), etc.

Bank jobs involve handling banking operations. These include deposits, loans, and client service. Bank jobs offer stable careers with good pay, allowances, and benefits. Bank employees are hired through examinations like IBPS PO, IBPS Clerk, SBI PO, SBI Clerk, RBI Grade B, RBI Assistant, etc.

Above are the few popular government career option available. You can find more career options on the National Career Service portal (ncs.gov.in) and Employment News (employmentnews.gov.in). They offer many opportunities and career choices for people.

Recruitment Agencies for Government of India

There are several central government agencies in India that conduct examinations for recruitment. Here are some of the most popular ones:

1. Union Public Service Commission (UPSC): It conducts exams and interviews. These are for hiring for the various civil services of the Government of India. Following are the exams conducted by UPSC.

- Combined Medical Services Examination
- Indian Forest Service Examination
- National Defence Academy and Naval Academy Examination
- Engineering Services Examination
- Central Armed Police Forces Examination
- Combined Defence Services Examination
- Central Bureau of Investigation
- Indian Economic Service and Indian Statistical Service Examination
- Civil Services Examination
- Geologist Examination and Combined Geo-Scientist Examination

2. **Staff Selection Commission (SSC):** It conducts examinations for recruitment to various Group B and Group C posts. These posts are in central government departments and ministries. Following are the various examinations conducted by SSC

· SSC CGL – Combined Graduate Level

· SSC GD – Constable, General Duty

· SSC CHSL – Combined Higher Secondary Level

· SSC JE – Junior Engineer

· SSC CPO – Central Police Organisation

· SSC MTS – Multitasking Staff

· SSC Stenographer 'C' and 'D'

· SSC JHT – Junior Hindi Translator

3. **Railway Recruitment Board (RRB):** It conducts examinations for recruitment to various posts in the Indian Railways, including the Group C and Group D posts.

4. **Institute of Banking Personnel Selection (IBPS):** It conducts examinations for recruitment to various posts in public sector banks in India.

5. **Defense Research and Development Organization (DRDO):** It conducts examinations for recruitment to various technical and administrative posts in the Defense sector.

In this chapter I have tried to include many career possibilities in Government Sector. However, there are many more job opportunities available in this sector from various state government, institutions and their companies that I must have missed.

I would urge you to explore more from Employment News websites or state government job portals.

Conclusion

When you started reading this book, you have read the promise I made to you. That is, you will be able to make a career decision if you follow this guide sincerely.

You started with understanding what a career means, why it is important to know what success means to you and how it impacts your career.

Then we explored various influences on career decisions and what a right career looks like. We gained insights into profession, passion, potential and A Right Career.

A free career assessment test scientifically helped you learn more about your career interests. Finally, we began our journey into Deciding a career wisely.

I believe that each of the steps that you followed in this book has brought some value to you. And I hope I was able to deliver on the promise I made in the beginning of this book.

Well done for Wisely Choosing a Career.

All the best for your future.

9 798894 754383